at sunrise,

Bird up
singing

by Ma

illustrated b

SIMON SPOTL
An imprint of Simon & Schuster Chil
1230 Avenue of the Americas, New
This Simon Spotlight edition
Text copyright © 2020 by Mar
Illustrations copyright © 2020 by L

For information about special discounts for bulk purch
Simon & Schuster Special Sales at 1-866-506-1949 or business
Manufactured in the United States of America 0
2 4 6 8 10 9 7 5 3 1
Library of Congress Cataloging-in-Publication D
Names: Singer, Marilyn, author. | Semple, Lucy, illust
Title: Bird singing, bird winging / by Marilyn Singer ; illustrated
Description: Simon Spotlight edition. | New York : Simon Spotl
Series: Ready-to-read. Pre-level one | Audience: Ages 3 - 5. | Summary: "C
different kinds singing, winging, walking, talking and so much more in this
book that includes a special section at the back of the book with facts on ea
Provided by publisher. Identifiers: LCCN 2019041528 | ISBN 9781534441439
ISBN 9781534441422 (paperback) | ISBN 9781534441446 (ebook)
Subjects: LCSH: Birds—Juvenile literature. | Birds—Behavior—Juvenile lite
Classification: LCC QL676.2 .S568 2020 | DDC 598—dc23
LC record available at https://lccn.loc.gov/2019041528

Bird getting hungry,
winging.

Bird on a tree trunk,
tapping.

Bird at a flower,
lapping.

Bird in a barnyard, scratching.

Bird by the river,
catching.

Bird in the grassland,
walking.

Bird in the playroom, talking.

Bird in the ocean,
diving.

Bird on the ice,
surviving.

Bird in the air,
playing.

Bird in a zoo,
displaying.

Bird with four eggs,
tending.

Bird with four chicks, defending.

Bird by a mudflat,
preening.

Bird in a birdhouse,
cleaning.

Bird in late summer,
waiting.

Bird in the fall,
migrating.

BIRD FACTS

All birds are two-legged animals with feathers. These feathers may be brightly colored or plain. Some males may be flashier to attract females. Some females may be plainer so they can hide more easily when they are raising chicks. All species of birds lay eggs, and some—but not all—can fly. They have bills or beaks to get food and eat, to groom, to defend themselves, and to communicate. Birds are excellent communicators. They use songs, calls, and other sounds, as well as movements, to talk to their mates and chicks, as well as other birds and animals.

Some birds migrate in the spring and fall, traveling to other areas to find food, escape rough weather, and breed. They may fly short or long distances. Other birds are called *residents*—they stay put. What birds do you see all year long? Which are just passing through? A pair of binoculars will help you see many types of our winged friends. You may even want to make a list!

- **Northern cardinals** often sing in the early morning to claim territory and to call to their mates and their chicks. Like many other types of birds, males and females look different. The male is bright red and the female more pale brown to grayish brown, with red highlights.

- Male and female **blue jays** look the same. These early-morning risers have loud voices, and they can imitate other birds. This may help them to chase away enemies as well as competitors for food.

- **Woodpeckers** tap on trees with their strong bills to find insects to eat. They pull out these bugs with their long, sticky tongues. They also drum on wood to communicate with their mates.

- Tiny **hummingbirds** reach inside flowers with their long beaks and tongues to drink nectar. These birds can fly up, down, and backward and can even hover over plants. Their wings beat so fast that they make a humming sound.

- **Chickens** have long been raised by people for eggs and meat. They scratch the soil looking for seeds, insects, and other food just as their wild relatives do. They also kick up dust and bathe in it, which is their way of keeping clean.

• The **bald eagle** is a large bird of prey. It snatches fish out of rivers and lakes with its sharp claws, called *talons*. It also steals fish from other birds and even from mammals.

• The **ostrich** is the tallest and heaviest of all birds. It can't fly. It walks through the African grasslands. When it is threatened, it runs. An adult ostrich can reach a speed of over forty miles per hour.

• The **parakeet** is also known as a *budgie*. This playful bird can be taught to imitate speech and other sounds. One budgie was recorded repeating more than 1,700 words!

• Male **blue-footed boobies** do a funny-looking dance, showing off their brightly colored feet to attract mates. When they hunt fish, they fold their long wings and plunge from as high as eighty feet into the water.

• **Penguins** can't fly, but they can zoom underwater to catch fish and other prey. Antarctic penguins have a thick layer of fat and feathers to protect them from the cold.

• **Ravens** are smart birds that can solve puzzles and play tricks and games. In the air, they sometimes fly upside down. They may be showing off for mates. Or they may just be having fun.

• **Peacocks** (male peafowl) are definitely showing off when they fan out the beautiful, long feathers that cover their tails. The peahens (female peafowl) seem to prefer males with the longest and brightest feathers. Peafowl live in the wild, but they have also been kept in zoos and as pets for thousands of years.

• During the spring and summer in the Arctic, the female **snowy owl** lays three to eleven eggs in a nest on the ground. The male catches rodents for her and the chicks. Most owls hunt at night, but snowy owls are diurnal—they hunt during the daylight.

• Male **red-winged blackbirds** will attack to protect their nests and chicks. Each male may have several mates with several nests. He will sing and show off his bright red-and-yellow shoulders to attract females and to chase away other males.

• Birds *preen*—they nibble their feathers to clean and arrange them. **Flamingos** spend a lot of time in the water. So when they preen, they also spread oil on their feathers. This oil keeps their feathers soft and waterproof and adds to the birds' pink color, which they get from their food.

• Birds have to keep their nests clean too. **Bluebirds** nest in tree holes and also in bird boxes. After their eggs hatch, the parents carry the chicks' poop out of the nest and drop it far away.

• In the fall, the **blackpoll warbler** migrates from North America to South America. It flies for as many as three days over the Atlantic Ocean—the longest nonstop trip over water for any songbird.

• **Snow geese** also fly south for the winter. These big birds travel in large, noisy flocks, while the small blackpoll warblers travel alone. In the spring, the geese will head back to the Arctic and nearby areas to breed.